More Little Hidden Pictures

Tony & Tony Tallarico

Dover Publication
Mineola, New Yor

International Standard Book Number

ISBN-13: 978-0-486-49337-4
ISBN-10: 0-486-49337-7

Manufactured in the United States by Courier Corporation
49337703   2014
www.doverpublications.com

NOTE

Get ready to look for balloons, aliens, bowling balls, pizza slices, and other hidden objects in the twenty-four picture puzzles in this fun-filled book. Each puzzle has a box on the bottom that shows you pictures of the objects to look for, as well as exactly how many of each one you will find. Color in each object as you find it—and count up the number of items when you're done. There's even a Solutions section after the puzzles, in case you need to check your answers. When you're done, you can color in all of the pages!

Find: 7 -

6 - 5 -

1 -

Everyone comes to watch the dancing fish!

2

Can you find the 23 objects
hidden in this picture?

These students work on art projects outside—
in the summer heat, and the winter snow!

4

Look carefully at this picture
to find 21 hidden objects.

You can ride this out-of this-world skateboard
all the way to outer space!

There are 20 objects hidden in this picture.
Can you find them all?

Find: 5- 🄑🄑🄑🄑🄑
◁◁◁◁◁ 3- 🚰🚰🚰 🏈🏈🏈
1- 🎳 🌙 🔦 🏏 👑 🌸 🧲 🍄 🪝 🪁

This batter *thought* he hit a homerun.

**Can you find the 25 objects
hidden in this picture?**

Find: 3- 1-

Who has the best costume at the
Halloween party?

There are 19 objects hidden in this picture.
Can you find them?

11

This adventurer has discovered a haunted cave.
Look out for ghosts!

**Can you find the 18 objects
hidden in this picture?**

Find:

7 -))))))))

5 - 🦴🦴🦴🦴🦴 2 - ⚙️⚙️ 🐟🐟

🎀🎀🎀 🕯️🕯️ 🎀 1 - 🍎 🎃 🍩

The human cannonball is
the star of this circus!

Look carefully at this picture
to find 26 hidden objects.

Find: 5-

3-

1-

These kids have a very special friend—
a dinosaur!

There are **30** objects hidden in this picture.
Can you find them all?

Find: 3- 🍄🍄🍄 👻👻👻 **-** ⌐

2- 🏠🏠 〰〰 ◇◇ 🧦🧦

1- 👓 🍎 🔦 ⌐ 🦴 ⛵ 🎵

Uh-oh! This fisherman has spotted
a crocodile!

**Look carefully at this picture to
find 21 hidden objects.**

19

Find:
7 -
6 - **3** - **2** -
1 -

This genie has the power to grant three wishes.
What will yours be?

There are 26 objects hidden in this picture.
Can you find them?

The clowns are trying to keep this
giant balloon from floating away!

Look carefully at this picture to
find 22 hidden objects.

Find: 6- 2- 1-

Here's Humpty Dumpty before his fall.

Can you find the 23 objects
hidden in this picture?

It's fun to ice skate on a snowy, winter day.

Look carefully at this picture to
find 16 hidden objects.

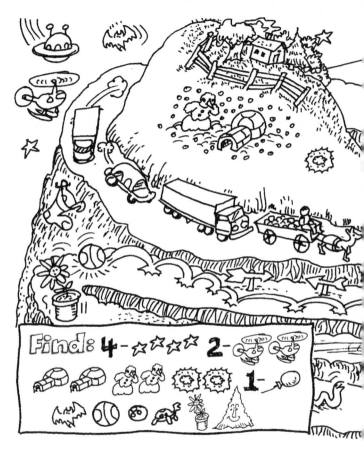

There are all kinds of people and vehicles
on the twisting mountain road.

There are 19 objects hidden in this picture.
Can you find them all?

Can you think of a plot for this crazy play?

Can you find the 24 objects hidden in this picture?

Find: 3- 🌽🌽🌽 ✏️✏️

2- 👡👡 🎐🎐 🎀🎀 😊😊

1- ⬅️ ☾ ⌒ 🍕 ⭐ 🥁 🍦

**What's better than pizza and a pool party
on a hot summer day?**

Look carefully at this picture to find 21 hidden objects.

Sometimes it's fun to play in the rain!

Can you find the 22 objects
hidden in this picture?

This band gets everyone in the mood to dance.

There are 21 objects hidden in this picture.
Can you find them all?

37

Find: 2- ✏️ 1- 🎻 🐦 🌸 🧤 🏈 🧦 🪖 🧢 🪚 🏮 🪁 ♥️ 🐩

These kids are on their way to school.

Look carefully at this picture to
find 15 hidden objects.

This is one crazy farm!
What would you grow on a farm?

Can you find the 29 objects hidden in this picture?

Find: 7 — [pencils]
2 — [egg, penguins, kites, stars] 1 — [lamb, bowl, mailbox, mug, sailboat, bone, shovel, pumpkin]

There are some interesting characters
on this ski slope.

There are 23 objects hidden in this picture.
Can you find them all?

Find: 2- ♡♡ ☆☆ ♫♫ ◉◉
1-

These people have come to this diner
to escape the rain.

Look carefully at this picture to
find 20 hidden objects.

Find: 3- ◇◇◇ 🐦🐦🐦 ☆☆☆ 🐢🐢🐢 2- ✏️✏️ 1- 👜 🌸 🍬 🐷 🫖 ⛸️

People gather to watch this
happy train speed by.

Can you find the 20 objects
hidden in this picture?

The great wizard uses his wand to
conjure up all sorts of things.

There are **25 objects** hidden in this picture.
Can you find them all?

49

SOLUTIONS

pages 2–3

pages 4–5

pages 6–7

pages 8–9

pages 10–11

pages 12–13

pages 14–15

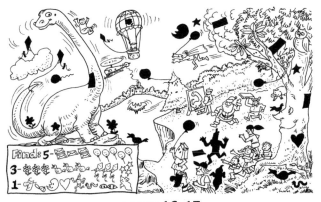

pages 16–17

Find: 3 -
2 -
1 -

pages 18–19

Find: 7 -
6 - 3 - 2 -
1 -

pages 20–21

pages 22–23

pages 24–25

pages 26–27

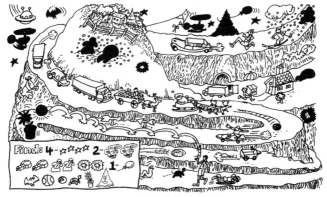

pages 28–29

pages 30–31

pages 32–33

pages 34–35

pages 36–37

pages 38–39

pages 40–41

pages 42–33

pages 44–45

pages 46–47

pages 48–49